Kid's Church Resource
Based on
Kai – Born to be Super
By Joy Vee

BROAD PLACE
publishing

First Published in Great Britain 2022

Broad Place Publishing
83 Nettleham Road
Lincoln
LN2 1RU

Copyright © Joy Velykorodnyy 2022

The author has asserted her rights under Section 77 of the Copyright, Designs and Patents Act, 1988, to be identified as the author of the work.
Images provided by Andru Keel and Canva.com

All rights reserved.

Scriptures taken from the Holy Bible, New International Version®, NIV®. Copyright © 1973, 1978, 1984, 2011 by Biblica, Inc.™ Used by permission of Zondervan. All rights reserved worldwide. www.zondervan.com The "NIV" and "New International Version" are trademarks registered in the United States Patent and Trademark Office by Biblica, Inc.™

Scripture quotations marked NLT are taken from the Holy Bible, *New Living Translation*, copyright 1996, 2004. Used by permission of Tyndale House Publishers, Inc., Wheaton, Illinois 60189. All rights reserved.

Kids' Church Resource based on Kai – Born to be Super
ISBN: 978-1915-034090

Extracts of *Kai – Born to be Super* used with permission.

Kai – Born to be Super
Paperback: ISBN 978-1915-034021
EBook: ISBN 978-1915-034120
Audiobook: ISBN 978-1915-034045

Joy would like to thank Chantelle Claxton, Tom Gawne and Nikki Salt for their input and feedback.

Welcome to this exciting new resource!

Dear Children's Worker,

I have created this six-week programme to help you with your small group or children programme. It's been designed for churches or small group
    a) That may have multiple ages together in Kids' Church
    b) That want to see their children grow in the things of God

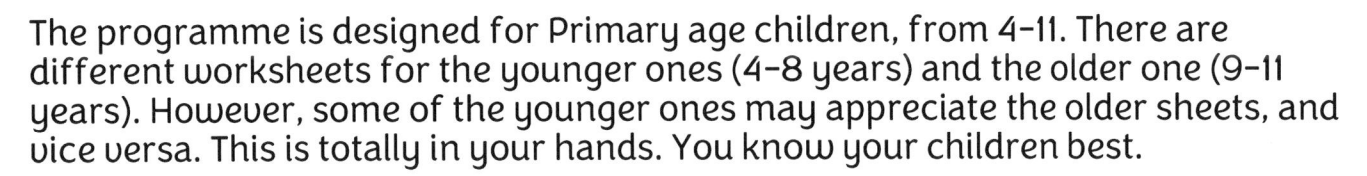

The programme is designed for Primary age children, from 4-11. There are different worksheets for the younger ones (4-8 years) and the older one (9-11 years). However, some of the younger ones may appreciate the older sheets, and vice versa. This is totally in your hands. You know your children best.

Most of the learning takes place in small groups. I recommend these be split into age groups, with younger ones having the option to do a craft if they finish talking before the older ones. It works best if the groups can be quite small – around 4-5 children. You may need more helpers. Could you ask a couple of the parents or members of the church's youth group to help out with the group-work? Some of the topics may not be easy – we are looking at being real and honest – so please choose people who love Jesus and will be able to pray with the children.

The programme is based on *Kai - Born to be Super*, a Christian fiction book written for 6-9-year-olds. The paperback book can be found anywhere books are sold, although they can be ordered in bulk from www.joyvee.org. There is also an audiobook, which is available on Google Play Books or direct from www.joyvee.org.

Each week has several pages of activities, including:
An icebreaker,
An opening thought,
A game (or two),
Deep thoughts (which can be read out)
Group work,
Story time,
Worship time (live or from Youtube)
Craft (for younger ones)
Worksheets
and a Sending Out blessing.

Choose what works best for your children, and feel free to add other things. See this resource as a buffet you can pick from!

Photocopiable pages start on page 27 or can be downloaded free of charge from www.joyvee.org.

I pray these resources will be a blessing for you and the children you serve.

Joy Vee xx

Kai – Born to be Super
Week 1

God Created Us for a Purpose
Bible Passage: Ephesians 2:10

On the next four pages are a range of activities. Choose the most appropriate ones to do with your children.

This first week, we are looking at lessons from Chapters 1-3 of *Kai – Born to be Super*. We will see that God created us for a unique purpose and He empowers us for that.

Prepare in advance:
Helpers at a ratio of 4-6 children per helper.
A4 Paper, markers and Blu-tac for Icebreaker.
For Game 1 – Different coloured markers and pads of sticky notes. (Post-its)
For Game 2 – Cut up Teacher's Sheet 1 or print out your own ideas.
For the Craft – purchase blank superhero masks for the children to decorate.
PHOTOCOPY: Group Questions Week 1 – Enough for each group to have a copy.
          Worksheet 1.1 & 1.2
          Teacher's Sheet 1
          Parents Letter Week 1

Icebreaker (5 mins):
What Super-Skills can you think of? Super-speed? Super-sight? Super-strength?
As children give you their ideas, write each idea on a separate piece of A4 paper, and have someone hang them round the room if you plan to play Game 1.

Opening Thought (5 mins):
How would your life be different if you had super-powers? Do you ever think about that, or find yourself wishing that you did?
Over the next six weeks, we will be looking at how we were Born to be Super, and how knowing Jesus can change our lives and make us *SUPER*.
There are lots of programmes on TV about people or animals with super-powers – Can you think of any?
Why do you think people enjoy these programmes?
Everyone, deep down, has the desire to have super-powers, to be able to do and be something extraordinary. Just think - how many people we could help if you had a special power?
For example, if I had super-hearing (this is a tricky one!), how could I use that to help people? *Have the children give you their ideas.*

Game 1 (10 mins):

Split the children into mixed-age teams of 5-8 people. (If you have a small number – it will work with teams of 2-3)
Each team will have a different coloured pen or block of sticky notes.
Two people in each group will be runners, and one or two can be writers.

Runner 1 – run to the wall, choose a super-power *(the ones you have hung up after the icebreaker)*, and run back and tell your team.

The team – work together to write down ways you could use that power to help people – One idea on each post-it note.

Runner 2 – run and stick the post-it notes on the paper with that power on, while **Runner 1** runs to find another super-power on the wall, and it continues.

You will get 1 point for each idea, but 2 points for each original idea that no other team thought of.

The game will continue for 7 or 8 minutes.

After the activity, ask one of the helpers, or some of the older children, to read out a few of the ideas from each super-power sheet.

During the next section, a helper can count the coloured slips and allocate points to have a winning team at the end.

Game 2 (10 mins):

Everyone is given a slip of a paper with a unique instruction/purpose- written on (*ideas below, but feel free to add your own!*).
Everyone must complete their action, then sit in an allocated corner or part of the room.
Rewards for everyone who can achieve their purpose in, for example, 3 minutes.
If you want, the slips can be redistributed to play again.

Ideas of instructions: (These, and more, are on Teacher's Sheet 1 – but feel free to create your own)
Run around the room 3 times / ask your teacher three questions and wait for their answers / introduce yourself to someone you don't know very well / etc

Deep Thoughts (5-10 mins): (Read aloud to the children)

We have looked at ideas for super-powers. Does anyone have any? Can anyone fly? Does anyone have super-strength?

Even though we don't have these super skills, I want to let you into a secret...

You were born to be SUPER.

God has a special purpose for your life, and He will give you the unique skills you need to complete that purpose. It's like having super-powers. Other people may be able to do the same things you do, but because it is part of your God-given purpose, it has more impact that someone else doing it.

Your skills + God's Purpose = Superpower Impact

Can you think of any of your skills which can be used in God's purpose?

Let's look at a verse from the Bible:

For we are God's masterpiece. He has created us anew in Christ Jesus, so we can do the good things he planned for us long ago. Ephesians 2:10 (NLT)

When you hear the word 'masterpiece' what do you think of? Is it something thrown together with little thought, or something worked on over a long time? *(Perhaps, as an illustration, show a quickly hand drawn picture of sunflowers compared to Van Gogh's version)*

Why did He work on us and create us as a 'masterpiece'?
To do good things – Our purpose.

And **how** did He do that?
He created us anew in Christ Jesus.

Group Work (10 mins):

Try to keep groups of a similar age, small enough to let everyone have a say. If possible, have a helper with each group, or have a helper gather a couple of groups together after 5 minutes to discuss their answers with them. We are not looking to lead the children in any direction, just to reflect on this and come to their own conclusions based on where they are.

Discuss these questions in your groups:
1) Do you feel like you have a purpose? If so, what do you think it is?
2) How does it make you feel to think that God has a special purpose for your life that only you can achieve, and He has given you the ability to achieve it?
3) What could stop you achieving this purpose?
4) How can you pray this week in the light of all we've discussed? (Just a 1 or 2 sentence prayer that you can remember.)

If possible, write the prayers on the wall, so everyone can see all the different prayers from all the groups.

Kai Story (10-15 mins) – Optional
Read Chapters 1-3 of Kai – Born to be Super.
Ask the children the questions at the end of the book after each chapter.

Craft time for younger ones (5-10 mins) – Optional
Can you design a superhero mask or cape?
How will this superhero help people?

Worship time (5-10 mins) – Optional
Here are some suggestions of songs you could sing / play, or use songs your children already know.
You make me brave – Hillsong Kids
Jesus is my superhero – Hillsong Kids
How great is our God – Chris Tomlin

Worksheets (5-10 mins) – Optional
The worksheets can be taken home for children to complete.
For the younger children (age 4-8)
Worksheet 1.1.
Encourage them to draw themselves as a superhero in the centre and write or draw their skills in the side areas.
For older children (age 8-11)
Worksheet 1.2
This is a journalling exercise, helping them process what was discussed in the group time.

Sending out (2 mins)
As the lesson ends, take a moment to pray for the children, that God will show them what their purpose is at this time, in the school / place they go every day.

Point out the prayers on the wall from the group session. Encourage them to remember one and pray it every day!
Remember to send the Parents' Letter home.

Kai – Born to be Super
Week 2

> On the next four pages are a range of activities. Choose the ones most appropriate to do with your children.

God is with us in difficult times
Bible Passage: Isaiah 43:1-2

This week we are looking at lessons from Chapters 4-5 of *Kai – Born to be Super*. We will see that God promises to be with us always, even in difficult times.

WARNING: This topic may be triggering for some children – there may be difficult questions about why God doesn't feel close in their situation. Please spend time praying for your children the week before and get a fresh word to share with children in these difficult situations.

Prepare in advance:
Helpers at a ratio of 4-6 children per helper.
For Game 1 – 2 small wagons or trollies. Lots of items (toys etc)
For Game 2 – Lots of different sized boxes.
For the Craft – Cut out a box template for each child.
PHOTOCOPY: Group Questions Week 2 – Enough for each group to have a copy.
          Worksheets 2.1 & 2.2
          Parents' Letter Week 2

Icebreaker (5 mins):
If you have access to a computer, show an Epic Fail Video on Youtube, stopping after a second or two, to ask what will go wrong. Play the video to check if you are right.
Or show photos from magazines, what is going to happen – how could it go wrong. (For example, a photo of some people getting married, a photo of a child riding a bike, a photo of a person walking a dog etc.)

Opening Thought (5 mins):
Last week, we looked at how our lives would be different if we had superpowers that could help people. This week, we are going to look at what happens when things go wrong – and they do! Sometimes, it's someone's fault; sometimes it's no one's fault.
We are going to see that even when things go wrong – But God is always with us.

Game 1 (10 mins):

Split into teams of 3 - 5 children (Min 2, max 5). Each group will need something with wheels (a large toy truck, a push along toy, etc) and a number of things to add on top (preferably soft, so no one gets hurt – toys, bean bags, shapes.)

Each team must load the vehicle, and then 1 person has to push / pull it across the room, racing with the other teams, while the rest of the team stays at the start line. The team that carries everything across fastest – wins.

If something drops off – it's back to the beginning and another person in the team becomes the puller / pusher.

The aim is that they cannot do it! So, make the carrying part so small and the carried objects so bulky it just can't work.

After 3-4 minutes stop the game.

How was that?
What did that feel like to the people watching?
How did that feel for the person pulling / pushing?

OK, we are going to do it again, but this time, the other team members are allowed to walk alongside! They can stop the pieces falling off. Nothing is allowed to fall off the wheels, but the team can 'help' hold it on!

Repeat the question:
How did that feel?

Game 2 (10 mins):

This is a variation of Game 1 – Only play one of them.

Have the children work together to create a winding path to walk along. Encourage them to make it quite difficult, with narrow spaces.

Now choose a volunteer. Stack the empty boxes into their arms, so they cannot see around it. Make them walk the path, without dropping any boxes. No one can give instructions of shout out help.

Again, the aim is for it to be very difficult or impossible.

Does another volunteer want to try?

When they have finished (or been disqualified for stepping off the path or dropping a box), ask them:
How did that feel?
How could it be easier?
What did that feel like to the people watching?

We will do it again, except this time, the volunteer can choose a friend who will give them directions and help.

Repeat the question:
How did that feel?

Deep Thoughts (5 mins): (Read aloud to the children)

In the game, was it difficult or easy to finish first time? Was it easier second time? Why? Things do go wrong, sometimes things pile up on us in life, and we are just not able to handle it all. Can you think of some of the things that pile on us and make life difficult? *Take ideas from the children.*

In those difficult times, there is an important truth I want you to remember:

God is with us!

The circumstances and your feelings are not the final word on the issue. God has something to say in those times. Let's look at a verse from the Bible:

But now, O Jacob, listen to the Lord who created you. O Israel, the one who formed you says, "Do not be afraid, for I have ransomed you. I have called you by name; you are mine.

² When you go through deep waters, I will be with you.

When you go through rivers of difficulty, you will not drown.

When you walk through the fire of oppression,

you will not be burned up; the flames will not consume you." Isaiah 43: 1-2

In which three situations does God promise to be close to us?
Deep waters, rivers of difficulty, fire of oppression
Why? (The answer is hidden in the first verse)
He created and formed us, then ransomed us – we are His.

It is important that we understand that God's truth is bigger than our feelings. Our feelings are valid, but they are not more important or more true than God's word. If I have to choose between what God says about a situation and how I feel about it – I must choose what God says (if I don't, my feelings get too much for me!) But this is not always easy!

Group Work (10-15 mins):

Try to keep groups small and of a similar age. We are not looking to lead the children in any direction, just to reflect on this and come to their own conclusions based on where they are.

If you feel able to discuss these questions in your groups and spend a bit of time praying for each other:

1) Do you have a story of God being close to you (or someone you know) in a difficult time?
2) In difficult times, it's hard to remember that God is with us. How can we remind ourselves that God is with us? *(Encourage practical ideas, such as journaling, writing scripture on post-its etc)*
3) How can you pray this week in the light of all we've discussed? (Just a 1 or 2 sentence prayer that you can remember.)
4) Do you wish to share of a personal experience you (or someone you know) is going through right now, so the group can pray for you?

If possible, write the prayers on the wall, so everyone can see and be encouraged.

Kai Story (5-10 mins) – Optional
Recap what happened last week in the story. Read Chapters 4-5 of *Kai – Born to be Super*. Ask the children the questions at the end of the book after each chapter.

Craft time for younger ones (5-10 mins) – Optional
Have the children decorate and make the boxes. They can put Bible Verses in, to help them when life is difficult.

Worship time (5-10 mins) – Optional
Here are some suggestions of songs you could sing / play, or use songs your children already know. (I think this time is important this week – because it's not an easy topic.)
You're Still God – Philippa Hanna
Another in the Fire – Hillsong United
It is Well – Bethel Music and Kristene Dimarco

Worksheets (5-10 mins) – Optional
The worksheets can be taken home for children to complete.
For the younger children (age 4-8) Worksheet 2.1.
Have them draw a tricky situation. Let them tell you about it, if they are able. Then encourage them to add Jesus to the picture. If they don't know where to add Him, spend a moment praying with them. *Jesus, can you show us, where were you at this time?*
For older children (age 8-11) Worksheet 2.2
This is a comprehension exercise, helping them take note of the scriptural promises, then giving them the chance to apply it practically.

Sending out (2 mins)
As the lesson ends, take time to pray with children who have said they feel like they are going through a difficult time.

Remind them of the prayers they came up with in group time and encourage them to remember one and pray it every day.
Remember to send the Parents' Letter home.

Kai – Born to be Super
Week 3

God wants to speak to us
Bible Passage: John 16:13-14

> On the next four pages are a range of activities. Choose the ones most appropriate to do with your children.

This week we are looking at lessons from Chapters 6-8 of *Kai – Born to be Super*. We will start to learn how God can speak to us.

This is a huge topic, and we are only touching on it this week. If your children want to learn more, I recommend *The Treasure Man* by Joy Vee.

Prepare in advance:
Helpers at a ratio of 4-6 children per helper.
For the Craft – Strips of card and circles – make headphones
PHOTOCOPY: Group Questions Week 3a **OR** Week 3b – Enough for each group to have a copy
　　　　　　Worksheets 3.1 & 3.2
　　　　　　Parents Letter Week 3

Icebreaker (5 mins):
What are the different ways you can communicate…
　　… with someone in the same room as you?
　　… with someone in the next room?
　　… with someone in another country?
　　… with someone in space?

Opening Thought (5 mins):
This week we are going to learn some of the ways God speaks to us.
Remember we learned that God has a purpose for our lives?
How will we know what that is, unless He tells us?
So, we are going to look at a few of the ways He talks to us, and practise listening to Him.

Game (10 mins):

Line the children up, one behind each other, facing in one direction – so everyone is looking at their neighbours' back.

Explain:

When someone taps your shoulder, you turn around, watch their actions.

They will tap you on the shoulder again when they have finished.

You then turn around, tap the shoulder of the person next in line, repeat the action, then tap their shoulder.

They will show the next person and so on.

This game will be played in silence.

At the end, have the first and last people in the line repeat their actions for everyone to see.

The action should be something clear, but not obvious! Maybe getting in a car, putting on your seatbelt, checking the mirror, then starting the car. Or getting on a motorbike and starting it up and driving round some bends in the road. Or anything else you can think of!

Kai Story (5-10 mins) – Optional

Recap what happened last week in the story. Read Chapters 6-8 of *Kai – Born to be Super*. Ask the children the questions at the end of the book after each chapter.

Craft time for younger ones (5-10 mins) – Optional

Decorate the strip and circles, then stick the circles at the end of the strip, to make headphones.

Worship time (5-10 mins) – Optional

Here are some suggestions of songs you could sing / play, or use songs your children already know.

Your Word O Lord – Resound Worship

Speak O Lord – Keith & Kristyn Getty

So Will I (100 Billion X) – Hillsong UNITED

Worksheets (5-10 mins) – Optional

The worksheets can be taken home for children to complete.

For the younger children (age 4-8) Worksheet 3.1.

Help the children read the worksheet – they can use drawing to answer the questions if they'd prefer.

For older children (age 8-11) Worksheet 3.2

This is a journalling exercise, although if God has spoken to them, they may prefer Worksheet 3.1 to help them remember.

Deep Thoughts (10 mins): (Read aloud to the children)

In the game we just played, what happened to the actions as it went from person to person? *It changed.*

That happens so much in life. We hear something, we tell someone, they change it a little, they tell someone else, changing it a little more. And it ends up totally different from what was first said.

God knows this happens – so He does something amazing. **He talks to us directly**. In the Bible there are lots of exciting ways God talked to people in the past (we could spend weeks and weeks looking at all the different ways), but now, **we have the Holy Spirit living in us** – and He talks to us directly.

Let's look at an example of this:

In Acts 27, Paul is on a journey by sea, that has had some problems. When they are at harbour, getting ready to set sail again, Paul says this:

"Men," he said, "I believe there is trouble ahead if we go on—shipwreck, loss of cargo, and danger to our lives as well." Acts 27:10

He said "I *believe*…" This is the word 'discern' or 'sense' – and he was right.

Sometimes the Holy Spirit gives us thoughts about things.

TEACHER: If you have a personal story, please share this at this time. If you don't, you can always use the story Zoe shares at the beginning of Chapter 7 of Kai – Born to be Super – Teacher's Sheet 3 (An even better idea – in the week before you teach, ask God to speak to you about something, so you have a fresh story to share with the children!)

When God speaks to us through our thoughts – it's not a magic trick, where we can ask God for whatever we want, and He tells us. (He won't give you the phone number of the person you like a school!) **He tells us the things that are important to Him**.

Let's read another Bible verse – This is Jesus telling his disciples about the Holy Spirit.

When the Spirit of truth comes, he will guide you into all truth. He will not speak on his own but will tell you what he has heard. He will tell you about the future. [14] He will bring me glory by telling you whatever he receives from me. John 16:13-14

The Holy Spirit only says what He hears from Jesus and God. So, what He tells us will be:

- **Kind**
- **Peaceful** (it won't make us feel upset or angry)
- **Pointing us to Jesus** (it will never make someone or something more important than Jesus)

Can we remember these points? *(Maybe write them on the wall – to help children remember.)*

We are going to go into our small groups, and practise listening to God speaking to us. Remember, it's not a magic trick, and we are practising. This is a safe place. We might get something wrong, and that's OK, but we have to start somewhere.

Group Work (5-10 mins):

There are a couple of activations listed below, just choose the one that is most relevant for your group. Maybe, try this together as a team, before doing it with the children.

a) In pairs, quietly pray and ask God to give you a <u>song</u>, or <u>a line of a song</u>, for the other person. (It doesn't have to be Christian song) Remember the rules – **kind, peaceful, pointing to Jesus** – if the song isn't any of those, it may not be God talking to you, so ask for another song.
When you have a song, share it with your partner.
When they give you a song, if you don't know what God is saying through that, ask Him to show you what He wants to say to you through that song.
Pray for God's blessing on each other.

b) In pairs, quietly pray and ask God to give you <u>a character from the Bible</u> for the other person. Remember the rules – **kind, peaceful, pointing to Jesus**.
When you have a name, share it with your partner.
When they give you a name, if you don't know what God is saying through that, ask Him to show you what He wants to say. You may need to go home and read about that person in the Bible.
Pray for God's blessing on each other.

Do any of you want to share in the group what song you were given and what it means to you?

Try to keep groups of a similar age, and small enough so there are 2 or 3 pairs in the each group. IT IS IMPORTANT IN THIS SESSION THAT THERE IS A HELPER IN EACH GROUP.

Sending out (2 mins)

Take the time to encourage those who didn't 'hear' anything. Pray with them and encourage them.
Ask them when they could 'practise' listening to God this week (for themselves, not necessarily for other people!).
Remember to send the Parents' Letter home.

Kai – Born to be Super
Week 4

> On the next four pages are a range of activities. Choose the ones most appropriate to do with your children.

Talking about Jesus with our friends
Bible Passage: 1 Peter 3:15

This week we are looking at lessons from Chapters 9-11 of *Kai – Born to be Super*. We will look at how we can talk to our friends about Jesus.

Prepare in advance:
Helpers at a ratio of 4-6 children per helper.
For Game 1 – slips of paper with names of famous people / characters.
For Game 2 – Large sheets of Flipchart Paper and pens.
For the Craft – Blank cards and sticker / pens to decorate
PHOTOCOPY: Group Questions Week 4 – Enough for each group to have a copy
                Worksheets 4.1 & 4.2
                Teacher's Sheet 4
                Parents Letter Week 4

Icebreaker (5 mins):
Try to tell each other what you had for dinner last night, or breakfast this morning, without using any words.
You can point to things, mine, draw – you just can't speak.
Have the children try to do it too.

Opening Thought (5 mins):
This week we are going to look at how we talk to our friends about Jesus.
Often when we try to talk about Jesus, it can be like we are using a totally different language. We have one idea of who we are talking about, but our friends often have a totally different idea.

      How can we talk about Jesus in a way that doesn't seem weird?

And what do we do if people still think Jesus is weird when we've finished talking to them.

Game 1 (10 mins):
In pairs, take a piece of paper. On it is a name of someone famous. Come up with 5 different words that can describe that person.
For older groups, you could have some words that can't be used – like Taboo.
Read out your words and see if the others can guess who you are talking about.

(Ideas for names: Queen Elizabeth, Spiderman, Father Christmas, Queen Elsa from Frozen, Princess Charlotte of Cambridge. Etc)

Game 2 (10 mins):
In teams of 4 or 5, get two pieces of large paper (flip-chart size)
On one of them write 'How I see Jesus'.
On the other write 'How my friends see Jesus'.
Brainstorm your ideas as a group. You have 3 minutes on each piece of paper. Fill them in as much as you can.

Afterwards, take feedback from the groups, with the other teams cheering if they have the same idea.

Deep Thoughts (10 mins): (Read aloud to the children)
We are told in the Bible to:
Always be prepared to give an answer to everyone who asks you to give the reason for the hope that you have. But do this with gentleness and respect. 1 Peter 3:15

People have different ideas of Jesus. Some people think he was a good teacher. Others think he is a fictional, made-up character.
So how we talk to someone, depends on what they think of Jesus.

Let's look at Paul with two different groups of people.

The first group – in the Synagogue. What do you think they knew about God? *They knew God and served Him.*
Read Acts 9:20: **And immediately he began preaching about Jesus in the synagogues, saying, "He is indeed the Son of God!"**

In the second group, he is in Athens – a pagan city who do not know God.
Read Acts 17:22-24: **So Paul, standing before the council, addressed them as follows: "Men of Athens, I notice that you are very religious in every way, ²³ for as I was walking along I saw your many shrines. And one of your altars had this inscription on it: 'To an Unknown God.' This God, whom you worship without knowing, is the one I'm telling you about. ²⁴ "He is the God who made the world and everything in it. Since he is Lord of heaven and earth, he doesn't live in man-made temples.**

Do you see? Paul changed his approach depending on who he was talking to? Sometimes we need to do that. Talking to someone who thinks Jesus isn't a real person, is very different than talking with someone who used to go to church, but doesn't anymore.   CONTINUED…

Deep Thoughts (continued)

I'm going to read a bit of *Kai – Born to be Super*. Kai had a dream about Jesus. Before the dream, he thought Jesus was a dead man who lived a long time ago. Now he is asking Alison, who is a Kids' Church Leader, about Jesus. I want you to think – is she doing a good job explaining? Or how could she do it better?

Read the extract from Teachers Sheet 4 or from Kai – Born to be Super, chapter 9.

Group Work (10-15 mins):

Try to keep groups small enough so everyone can talk, and with children of a similar age if possible.

In your groups, talk about the following questions:
1) What did you think about how Alison answered the question?
2) How would you describe Jesus to someone who had never heard of him before?
3) How could you talk about Jesus with a friend who used to go to church, but doesn't anymore?
4) Alison made the story about sheep more real by talking about something Kai knew about – cats. Can you think of a story Jesus told, and change it to make it mean more to normal people today? Choose a story and work on it together.

Take time at the end to gather as a group and listen to each other's ideas and stories.

Kai Story (5-10 mins) – Optional

Recap what happened last week in the story. Read Chapters 9-11 of *Kai – Born to be Super*. Ask the children the questions at the end of the book after each chapter.

Craft time for younger ones (5-10 mins) – Optional

Have the children make and decorate a card they can give to their friend, telling their friend that Jesus loves them, or inviting them to Kids' Church.

Worship time (5-10 mins) – Optional
Here are some suggestions of songs you could sing / play, or use songs your children already know.
Jesus is my superhero – Hillsong Kids
Mighty to Save – Hilling Worship
Indescribable – Chris Tomlin

Sending out (2 mins)
What do we do when our friends don't want to hear about Jesus? We can still pray for them**! God can do a miracle in their heart, even without us saying anything.**
Pray for the friends God has put on your hearts together.
Remember to send the Parents' Letter home.

Worksheets (5-10 mins) – Optional
The worksheets can be taken home for children to complete.
For the younger children (age 4-8) Worksheet 4.1.
Let them colour in Kai, then add a drawing to help them remember the story they came up with in the group time.
For older children (age 8-11) Worksheet 4.2
This is a journalling exercise.

Kai – Born to be Super
Week 5

> On the next four pages are a range of activities. Choose the ones most appropriate to do with your children.

Sharing the Good News
Bible Passage: Romans 10:14

This week we are looking at lessons from Chapters 12-14 of *Kai – Born to be Super*. We will see how we can use our own stories (testimonies) and then share the good news of the gospel with our friends.

Prepare in advance:
Helpers at a ratio of 4-6 children per helper.
For Game 1 – See Teachers Sheet 5 or come up with your own example.
For the Craft – Blank cards and sticker / pens to decorate
PHOTOCOPY: Worksheets 5.1 & 5.2
     Teacher's Sheet 5
     Parents' Letter 5
OPTIONAL – Consider ordering a pack of '*Kai – Fulfilling his Purpose*' tracts so the children can take home the gospel message to share with a friend. Available from www.joyvee.org

Icebreaker (5 mins):
Make an announcement such as 'Big Ben is really only 2 metres tall, it's just the photos are taken at weird angles!' or 'The Eiffel Tower isn't really in Paris – it's just photoshopped into photos.'
As the children argue with you – ask them to prove what they are saying. *(Hopefully, one of them will come up with the fact that they have been there and seen it.)*
You might disagree with someone's point of view, but your arguments are disqualified by their experience.

Opening Thought (5 mins):
We looked last week at how to talk to our friends about Jesus. Some of them may not want to know and may even argue that Jesus is not real. But, if you know that Jesus is real, because you talk to Him, He talks to you, He answers your prayers. They might not like your stories, but they can't argue against your experience.
If your friends aren't sure about Jesus, you can tell them a story from your life about when He made a difference to you.

Game 1 (10 mins):

Using Teacher's Sheet 5, or create your own photo and sentences.
Split the children into two teams.
One person from each team is chosen as the artist, and the others are runners.
This is a relay race.
One team will look at the photo, the other will be given your sentences (and can't see the photo).
One member of each team runs to the front of the room, receives a slip of paper / looks at the photo, and returns to his team.
He reads / describes it to his team, who draw it, then the next person goes to get the next sentence / next description of the photo.
(The person describing the photo can only say 1 sentence/thing about the picture. The person drawing cannot be a runner and see the actual picture.)

At the end, compare the pictures with the actual photo.

Repeat with a different picture if you like.

The aim of the game is to show the difference between retelling a real experience (describing a photo) compared to sharing a second-hand experience (the sentences). Our own stories of God at work in our lives, are always powerful.

Game 2 (10 mins):

Ask one of the helpers to talk about a place they have been. They need to 'sell' the place to the children, telling them how wonderful it is.
After listening, ask the children how many people want to go there. Keep a tally.

Ask the children to think of somewhere exciting they have been.
Is there a volunteer who wants to tell us about their place?
Can you tell us about it, so we all want to go there too?

Have three or four people give examples of places they have been to.

Then ask if someone has ever been to China? Hawaii? Alaska? Mexico? Ask someone who **hasn't** been to one of those places to talk about it.
How many people want to go there?

Hopefully, unless you have a very charismatic child in your group, most people will want to go to places people have been to, as there will be more authenticity in their stories and retelling.

Kai Story (10 mins) – Optional

Read this week's story BEFORE the DEEP THOUGHT SECTION.
Recap what happened last week in the story.
Read Chapters 12-14 of *Kai – Born to be Super*.
Ask the children the questions at the end of the book after each chapter.

Craft time for younger ones (5-10 mins) – Optional

After (or as part of) the group work, have the children hold a bean bag, and remember something selfish or wrong they did. Lead them in a prayer to say sorry, then have then throw the bean bag as far away as they can.

Deep Thoughts (15 mins): (Read aloud to the children)

When we tell our stories, there may be someone listening who God has been talking to. God is always working, trying to get the attention of those who don't know Him. Maybe your story will be just what they need to hear. Today we are going to look at how to share the good news of Jesus, because unless we tell them, how will they know? Romans 10:14.

If someone says to you *'I want to know Jesus better. How do I do it?'*, here is what you can say:

- Everyone was born for something special, because God **created** them for a special purpose (remember our verse from week 1 – Ephesians 2:10)
- We can only find our true purpose when we are **close** to God – like best friends. So, everything you do with your friends, like laughing and chatting, that's what you do with God. That's living the life you were born to live.
- The problem is, we do **selfish** things and wrong things – these are called 'sins'. These sins build a **wall** between us and God, so we can't be close. We can't take the wall down, so how can we be close to God?
- God knew people are not strong enough to break down the wall, so He sent his Son, Jesus, to **smash** that wall – so we can get back to God.
- Jesus came and lived a perfect life, but then He died. The Bible says that He died as a **punishment** for all our sins – the wrong things we have done.
- But He didn't stay dead. He came **alive** again, smashing the wall, so we can be close friends with him.
- You can say a prayer to get close to Jesus again – like this one:

Dear Jesus, I'm sorry for all the bad things I did, the bricks that made a wall between us and stopped me being close to You. I don't want those things between us anymore. Thank you for coming and smashing the wall. I want to be your friend. I want to live my life with you. Amen

- Now, you can live your life close to Jesus! But it's **not easy** remembering Jesus every day, and we need extra help. So, Jesus sends us the **Holy Spirit** who lives in us and helps us remember Jesus and teaches us how to be His friend.
- You can pray a prayer like this:

Dear Jesus, Thank You for being my best friend. Please send the Holy Spirit into my life to help me live for You. Holy Spirit, please come into my life, Amen.

- Now you can live the life you were born to live.

(Take time to go over each step, explaining it further if the children need it, and allowing them to ask questions).

This gospel presentation is available in a tract called 'Kai-Fulfilling his Destiny' *available from* www.joyvee.org.

Group Work (5-10 mins):

In your groups, try to remember the steps together and practise telling each other. Can you think of a way to help you remember these points?

Does anyone in your group want to pray the prayer to become friends with Jesus – maybe for the first time, or maybe because you know there is a wall between you and God.
Pray for everyone in the group to have the Holy Spirit living in them.

Worship time (5-10 mins) – Optional

Here are some suggestions of songs you could sing / play, or use songs your children already know.
Greatest Day in History (Happy Day) – Tim Hughes
Mighty to Save – Hillsong Worship
Reckless Love – Cory Asbury

Worksheets (5-10 mins) – Optional

The worksheets can be taken home for children to complete.
For the younger children (age 4-8) Worksheet 5.1.
If the child feels comfortable, they can write on the bricks the things they know Jesus has forgiven them for.
For older children (age 8-11) Worksheet 5.2
This sheet is to help them remember the steps. Maybe have them try to remember and quiz each other.

Sending out (2 mins):

Encourage the children to tell someone today about how Jesus has a purpose for them, but sin can make a wall, but Jesus came to remove the wall so we can be close to God.
Don't worry if that person already knows Jesus. We can all let sin get in the way sometimes. Even grown-ups need reminding that we can come back to Jesus and be close to Him.
Pray for the children to have the right words to say.
Remember to send the Parents' Letter home.

Kai – Born to be Super
Week 6

> On the next three pages are a range of activities. Choose the ones most appropriate to do with your children.

THIS is my purpose!
Bible Passage: John 14:26

This week is based on Chapter 15 of *Kai – Born to be Super* and has a party-feel. We will talk about who the Holy Spirit is, and then pray, before moving on to party games and a celebration!

Prepare in advance:

Helpers at a ratio of 4-6 children per helper – *Spend time praying together before the children come in.*
Party Games and Party Food.
Craft supplies and paper to make a poster.
Ingredients to make ice cream sundaes.
PHOTOCOPY: Group Questions Week 4 – Enough for each group to have a copy
　　　　　Parents' Letter 6.
OPTIONAL – Consider ordering a pack of 'Kai – Fulfilling his Purpose' tracts so the children can take home the gospel message to share with a friend. Available from www.joyvee.org.

Icebreaker (2 mins):
Describe your favourite kind of ice cream. How do you like to eat it? In a cone, on a stick – like a magnum, in a bowl?

Opening Thought (5 mins):
Over the last 6 weeks, we have looked at how we find out purpose.
Who gave us our purpose? *God*
And how do we find it? *By being in Christ Jesus*
How to we make sure we are close to Jesus? *By asking Him to take down the wall of sin between us and Him.*
How do we remember to live for Him every day? *By asking the Holy Spirit to be with us.*

Deep Thoughts (10 mins): (Read aloud to the children)

I asked you earlier about ice cream and I want to use ice cream to explain something very important. We read about it last week, in the story of Kai. Do you remember? We are going to look at that a little more today to help you understand.

Sometimes, you or your friends might ask questions like:

> What's the difference between God and Jesus and the Holy Spirit?

We call this the Trinity. This word isn't in the Bible, but there are lots of places where we see all three together.

One example is **Genesis 1:1-3**. Can someone read it out?

We see God the Father (making the heavens and the earth), God the Holy Spirit (hovering over the water), but where is Jesus? What are the first three words in verse 3 – *And God said* – who is the Word of God? (*Look up John 1:1-3, 14.*)

Here's another example – See if you can see all three parts of the trinity:
Luke 3:21-22

Jesus tells his disciples to baptise people in the name of... See **Matt 28:9**

So, how does the Trinity work? It's so difficult for us to understand – But I have a way that helps me. **Ice cream!**

If we think of ice cream in a cone and ice cream in a bowl. They are both ice cream, aren't they? They are made of the same thing – they are just eaten in a different way.

Jesus and God the Father are both God. They have all the inside power of God, all the knowledge of God – they are both God. Just like ice cream in a cone and in a bowl are both ice cream. But they are in different shapes or forms. They have slightly different characteristics – but those differences don't stop them being the same God. It's not 2 gods – there is only 1 God. It is the same God, in different forms. It's complicated – but that's because our little human minds struggle to understand someone as big and amazing as God.

So, what about the Holy Spirit? Well, that's like the ice cream when it is in my stomach! It is the same God, but He is living inside of me!

Let's read our verse for this week:

> **The Holy Spirit, who the Father will send in my name, will teach you all things and will remind you of everything I have said to you.** John 14:26

Now we have the Holy Spirit inside us, He will teach us how to listen to God and live for God. We learn more about that in Kids' Church and from other Christians. We are always learning. And the more we learn from the Holy Spirit, the more we fulfil the purpose God put us on earth for.

Group Work (5-10 mins):

In your groups, take time to pray for each other. You can pray the prayer from last week, inviting the Holy Spirit to come in.

Dear Jesus, Thank You for being my best friend. Please send the Holy Spirit into my life to help me live for You. Holy Spirit, please come into my life, Amen.

Pray that you will learn how to listen to the Holy Spirit
Pray that you will get better and better at living the purpose God has for you
Pray that God will bring your way people you can tell about Him.

Kai Story (5 mins) – Optional

Recap what happened last week in the story.
Read Chapter 15 of *Kai – Born to be Super*.
Ask the children the questions at the end of the book after each chapter.
What was your favourite part of the story?
Has reading about Kai helped you learn more about Jesus?

Craft time for younger ones (5-10 mins) – Optional

Create a poster about *Kai – Born to be Super*!
Hang the poster somewhere people can see it!

Worship time (5-10 mins) – Optional

Here are some suggestions of songs you could sing / play, or use songs your children already know.
Holy Spirit (You are Welcome Here) – Jesus Culture
Spirit Break Out – Kim Walker-Smith

Ice cream (5-10 mins) – Optional

Create and enjoy an ice cream sundae today!

Games (15 mins):

One of the things God created us for was to enjoy Him. We are going to play party games and have food together, remembering that Jesus is here with us. As we play together, remember that He is here too, because He wants to be our best friend.
Ideas for games:
Musical Chairs.
Build a wall with plastic cups – knock it down with bean bags.
Charades – Mine out a job – the others have to guess what it is.
Create a tunnel of blessing for each other, and pray as they run through it.
Try another activation from Week 3.
Anything else you can think of!

Sending out (5 mins):

Gather the children and pray a blessing over them.
Ask if any of them would like to pray for you and the other helpers.
Tell them that you are always available for them, even outside Kids' Church time, to pray with them or help them. Remind them Jesus is always with us too, through His Holy Spirit.
Remember to send the Parents' Letter home.

Photocopiable Resources

Group Questions Week 1
Group Questions Week 2
Group Questions Week 3a
Group Questions Week 3b
Group Questions Week 4
Group Questions Week 6

Worksheets 1.1 & 1.2
Worksheets 2.1 & 2.2
Worksheets 3.1 & 3.2
Worksheets 4.1 & 4.2
Worksheets 5.1 & 5.2

Teacher's Sheet 1
Teacher's Sheet 3
Teacher's Sheet 4
Teacher's Sheet 5

Parents' Letters Week 1
Parents' Letters Week 2
Parents' Letters Week 3
Parents' Letters Week 4
Parents' Letters Week 5
Parents' Letters Week 6

Also available as a PDF from www.joyvee.org

Born to be Super – Week 1 Group Questions Week 1

Group Work (10 mins):

Discuss these questions in your groups:
1) Do you feel like you have a purpose? If so, what do you think it is?
2) How does it make you feel to think that God has a special purpose for your life that only you can achieve, and He has given you the ability to achieve it?
3) What could stop you achieving this purpose?
4) How can you pray this week in the light of all we've discussed? (Just a 1 or 2 sentence prayer that you can remember.)

If possible, write the prayers on the wall, so everyone can see all the different prayers from all the groups.

Group Work (10 mins):

Discuss these questions in your groups:
1) Do you feel like you have a purpose? If so, what do you think it is?
2) How does it make you feel to think that God has a special purpose for your life that only you can achieve, and He has given you the ability to achieve it?
3) What could stop you achieving this purpose?
4) How can you pray this week in the light of all we've discussed? (Just a 1 or 2 sentence prayer that you can remember.)

If possible, write the prayers on the wall, so everyone can see all the different prayers from all the groups.

Group Work (10 mins):

Discuss these questions in your groups:
1) Do you feel like you have a purpose? If so, what do you think it is?
2) How does it make you feel to think that God has a special purpose for your life that only you can achieve, and He has given you the ability to achieve it?
3) What could stop you achieving this purpose?
4) How can you pray this week in the light of all we've discussed? (Just a 1 or 2 sentence prayer that you can remember.)

If possible, write the prayers on the wall, so everyone can see all the different prayers from all the groups.

PHOTOCOPIABLE © www.joyvee.org

Born to be Super – Week 2 Group Questions Week 2

Group Work (10-15 mins):

If you feel able to discuss these questions in your groups and spend a bit of time praying for each other:

1) Do you have a story of God being close to you (or someone you know) in a difficult time?
2) In difficult times, it's hard to remember that God is with us. How can we remind ourselves that God is with us? *(Encourage practical ideas, such as journaling, writing scripture on post-its etc)*
3) How can you pray this week in the light of all we've discussed? (Just a 1 or 2 sentence prayer that you can remember.)
4) Do you wish to share of a personal experience you (or someone you know) is going through right now, so the group can pray for you?

If possible, write the prayers on the wall, so everyone can see and be encouraged.

Group Work (10-15 mins):

If you feel able to discuss these questions in your groups and spend a bit of time praying for each other:

1) Do you have a story of God being close to you (or someone you know) in a difficult time?
2) In difficult times, it's hard to remember that God is with us. How can we remind ourselves that God is with us? *(Encourage practical ideas, such as journaling, writing scripture on post-its etc)*
3) How can you pray this week in the light of all we've discussed? (Just a 1 or 2 sentence prayer that you can remember.)
4) Do you wish to share of a personal experience you (or someone you know) is going through right now, so the group can pray for you?

If possible, write the prayers on the wall, so everyone can see and be encouraged.

PHOTOCOPIABLE © www.joyvee.org

Born to be Super – Week 3   Group Questions Week 3a

Group Work (5-10 mins):

In pairs, quietly pray and ask God to give you a song, or a line of a song, for the other person. (It doesn't have to be Christian song) Remember the rules – **kind, peaceful, pointing to Jesus** – if the song isn't any of those, it may not be God talking to you, so ask for another song.

When you have a song, share it with your partner.

When they give you a song, if you don't know what God is saying through that, ask Him to show you what He wants to say to you through that song.

Pray for God's blessing on each other.

Do any of you want to share in the group what song you were given and what it means to you?

Group Work (5-10 mins):

In pairs, quietly pray and ask God to give you a song, or a line of a song, for the other person. (It doesn't have to be Christian song) Remember the rules – **kind, peaceful, pointing to Jesus** – if the song isn't any of those, it may not be God talking to you, so ask for another song.

When you have a song, share it with your partner.

When they give you a song, if you don't know what God is saying through that, ask Him to show you what He wants to say to you through that song.

Pray for God's blessing on each other.

Do any of you want to share in the group what song you were given and what it means to you?

Group Work (5-10 mins):

In pairs, quietly pray and ask God to give you a song, or a line of a song, for the other person. (It doesn't have to be Christian song) Remember the rules – **kind, peaceful, pointing to Jesus** – if the song isn't any of those, it may not be God talking to you, so ask for another song.

When you have a song, share it with your partner.

When they give you a song, if you don't know what God is saying through that, ask Him to show you what He wants to say to you through that song.

Pray for God's blessing on each other.

Do any of you want to share in the group what song you were given and what it means to you?

PHOTOCOPIABLE © www.joyvee.org

Born to be Super – Week 3 Group Questions Week 3b

Group Work (5-10 mins):

In pairs, quietly pray and ask God to give you a character from the Bible for the other person. Remember the rules – **kind, peaceful, pointing to Jesus**.

When you have a name, share it with your partner.

When they give you a name, if you don't know what God is saying through that, ask Him to show you what He wants to say. You may need to go home and read about that person in the Bible.

Pray for God's blessing on each other.

Do any of you want to share in the group what song you were given and what it means to you?

Group Work (5-10 mins):

In pairs, quietly pray and ask God to give you a character from the Bible for the other person. Remember the rules – **kind, peaceful, pointing to Jesus**.

When you have a name, share it with your partner.

When they give you a name, if you don't know what God is saying through that, ask Him to show you what He wants to say. You may need to go home and read about that person in the Bible.

Pray for God's blessing on each other.

Do any of you want to share in the group what song you were given and what it means to you?

Group Work (5-10 mins):

In pairs, quietly pray and ask God to give you a character from the Bible for the other person. Remember the rules – **kind, peaceful, pointing to Jesus**.

When you have a name, share it with your partner.

When they give you a name, if you don't know what God is saying through that, ask Him to show you what He wants to say. You may need to go home and read about that person in the Bible.

Pray for God's blessing on each other.

Do any of you want to share in the group what song you were given and what it means to you?

PHOTOCOPIABLE © www.joyvee.org

Group Work (10-15 mins):

In your groups, talk about the following questions:
1) What did you think about how Alison answered the question?
2) How would you describe Jesus to someone who had never heard of him before?
3) How could you talk about Jesus with a friend who used to go to church, but doesn't anymore?
4) Alison made the story about sheep more real by talking about something Kai knew about – cats. Can you think of a story Jesus told, and change it to make it mean more to normal people today? Choose a story and work on it together.

Take time at the end to gather as a group and listen to each other's ideas and stories.
Are there any ideas you want to write down to remember and maybe use in the next week or two when talking to your friends about Jesus?

Group Work (10-15 mins):

In your groups, talk about the following questions:
1) What did you think about how Alison answered the question?
2) How would you describe Jesus to someone who had never heard of him before?
3) How could you talk about Jesus with a friend who used to go to church, but doesn't anymore?
4) Alison made the story about sheep more real by talking about something Kai knew about – cats. Can you think of a story Jesus told, and change it to make it mean more to normal people today? Choose a story and work on it together.

Take time at the end to gather as a group and listen to each other's ideas and stories.
Are there any ideas you want to write down to remember and maybe use in the next week or two when talking to your friends about Jesus?

PHOTOCOPIABLE © www.joyvee.org

Group Work (5-10 mins):

In your groups, take time to pray for each other. You can pray the prayer from last week, inviting the Holy Spirit to come in.

Dear Jesus, Thank You for being my best friend. Please send the Holy Spirit into my life to help me live for You. Holy Spirit, please come into my life, Amen.

Pray that you will learn how to listen to the Holy Spirit

Pray that you will get better and better at living the purpose God has for you

Pray that God will bring your way people you can tell about Him.

Group Work (5-10 mins):

In your groups, take time to pray for each other. You can pray the prayer from last week, inviting the Holy Spirit to come in.

Dear Jesus, Thank You for being my best friend. Please send the Holy Spirit into my life to help me live for You. Holy Spirit, please come into my life, Amen.

Pray that you will learn how to listen to the Holy Spirit

Pray that you will get better and better at living the purpose God has for you

Pray that God will bring your way people you can tell about Him.

Group Work (5-10 mins):

In your groups, take time to pray for each other. You can pray the prayer from last week, inviting the Holy Spirit to come in.

Dear Jesus, Thank You for being my best friend. Please send the Holy Spirit into my life to help me live for You. Holy Spirit, please come into my life, Amen.

Pray that you will learn how to listen to the Holy Spirit

Pray that you will get better and better at living the purpose God has for you

Pray that God will bring your way people you can tell about Him.

Group Work (5-10 mins):

In your groups, take time to pray for each other. You can pray the prayer from last week, inviting the Holy Spirit to come in.

Dear Jesus, Thank You for being my best friend. Please send the Holy Spirit into my life to help me live for You. Holy Spirit, please come into my life, Amen.

Pray that you will learn how to listen to the Holy Spirit

Pray that you will get better and better at living the purpose God has for you

Pray that God will bring your way people you can tell about Him.

PHOTOCOPIABLE © www.joyvee.org

Born to be Super – Week 1   Worksheet 1.1

What skills do you have?

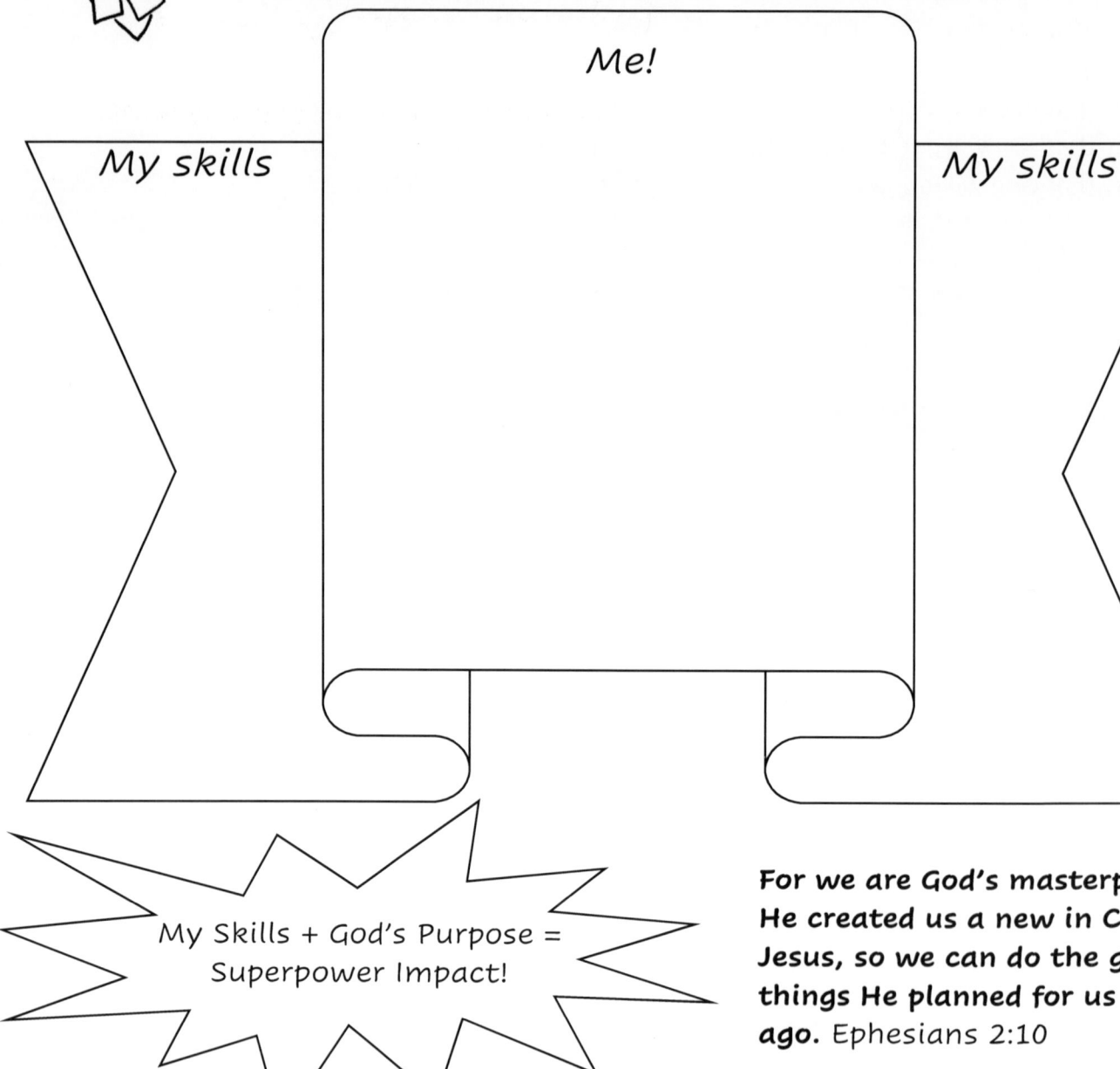

Me!

My skills   My skills

My Skills + God's Purpose = Superpower Impact!

For we are God's masterpiece. He created us a new in Christ Jesus, so we can do the good things He planned for us long ago. Ephesians 2:10

Write a prayer you want to remember to say this week:

PHOTOCOPIABLE © www.joyvee.org

My Skills + God's Purpose = Superpower Impact

My skills are:
_____
_____
_____
_____
_____

Skills I want to develop in the future:

What stops me using my skills?
_____
_____
_____
_____
_____

How can my skills help people?
- ♦
- ♦
- ♦
- ♦

For we are God's masterpiece. He created us a new in Christ Jesus, so we can do the good things He planned for us long ago. Ephesians 2:10

Born to be Super – Week 2　　　　　　　　　　　　　　　　　　　　　Worksheet 2.1

Does God really care?
Read Isaiah 43:1-2.

Draw yourself in a tricky situation:

Now draw Jesus with you, adding Him into the picture - Because He is with us, even when we can't see Him.

PHOTOCOPIABLE © www.joyvee.org

Born to be Super – Week 2   Worksheet 2.2

Does God really care?
Read Isaiah 43:1-2.

Where is He in the deep water?

Where is He in the river of difficulty?

Where is He in the fire?

Why?
Because He _____ us, He _____ us, He _____ us. We are _____.

Practical ideas to help me remember God is with me:

A prayer to remember this week:

PHOTOCOPIABLE © www.joyvee.org

Born to be Super – Week 3 Worksheet 3.1

God wants to speak to me and tell me what is important to Him.

What did God say to me in Kid's Church today?

What does that mean?

How can I remember that this week?

This space is to write down the things God speaks to me this week.

When the Spirit of truth comes, he will guide you into all truth. He will not speak on his own but will tell you what he has heard. John 16:13

PHOTOCOPIABLE © www.joyvee.org

Born to be Super – Week 3   Worksheet 3.2

God can speak to me through the Holy Spirit.

Some of the ways God speaks to me:

_____

_____

_____

_____

How can I practise listening to God this week?

A story from this week of God speaking to me:

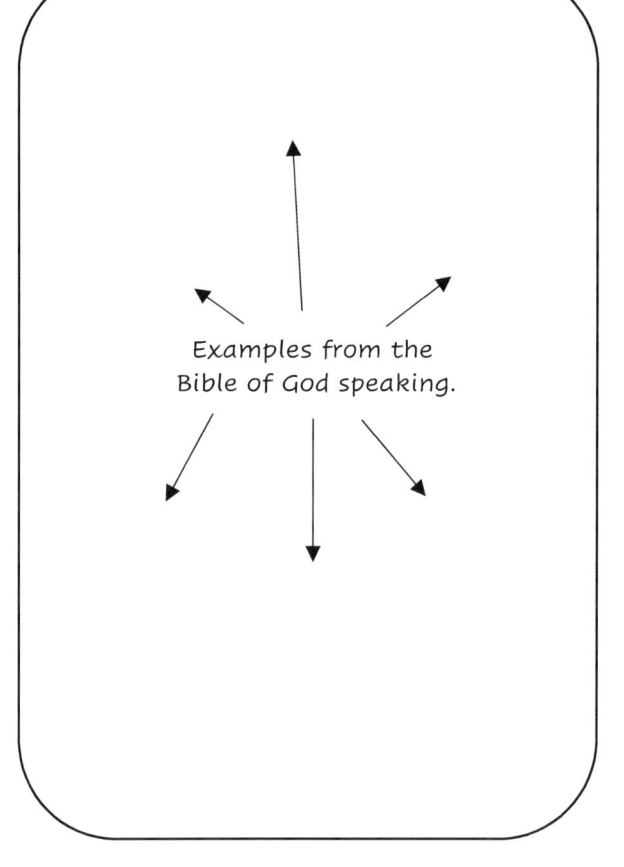

Examples from the Bible of God speaking.

When the Spirit of truth comes, he will guide you into all truth. He will not speak on his own but will tell you what he has heard. John 16:13

PHOTOCOPIABLE © www.joyvee.org

Born to be Super – Week 4

Worksheet 4.1

Alison told Kai a story about lots of cats.
Colour in Kai, then draw a picture to help you remember the new story you thought of in your group.

PHOTOCOPIABLE © www.joyvee.org

How can I describe Jesus?

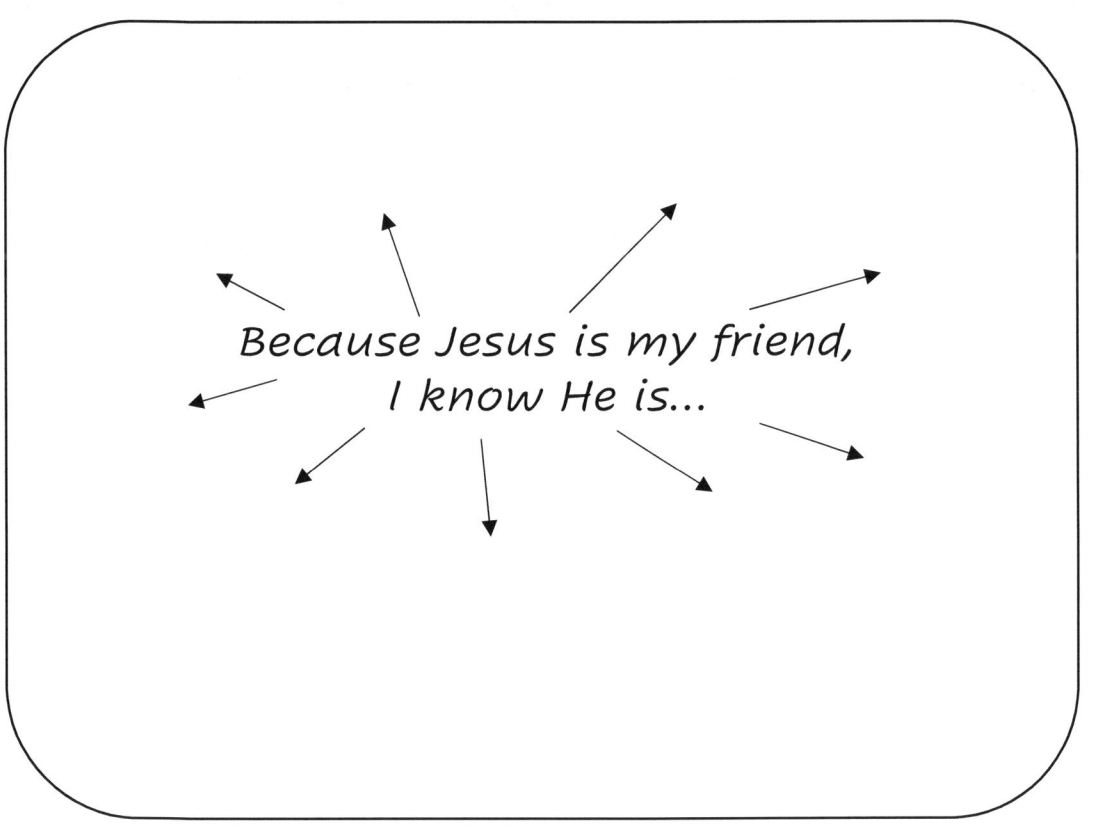

Because Jesus is my friend, I know He is...

My retelling of a story of Jesus – so that it makes sense to people today:

PHOTOCOPIABLE © www.joyvee.org

This brick wall separates us from Jesus. Every brick is something selfish or wrong we have done.

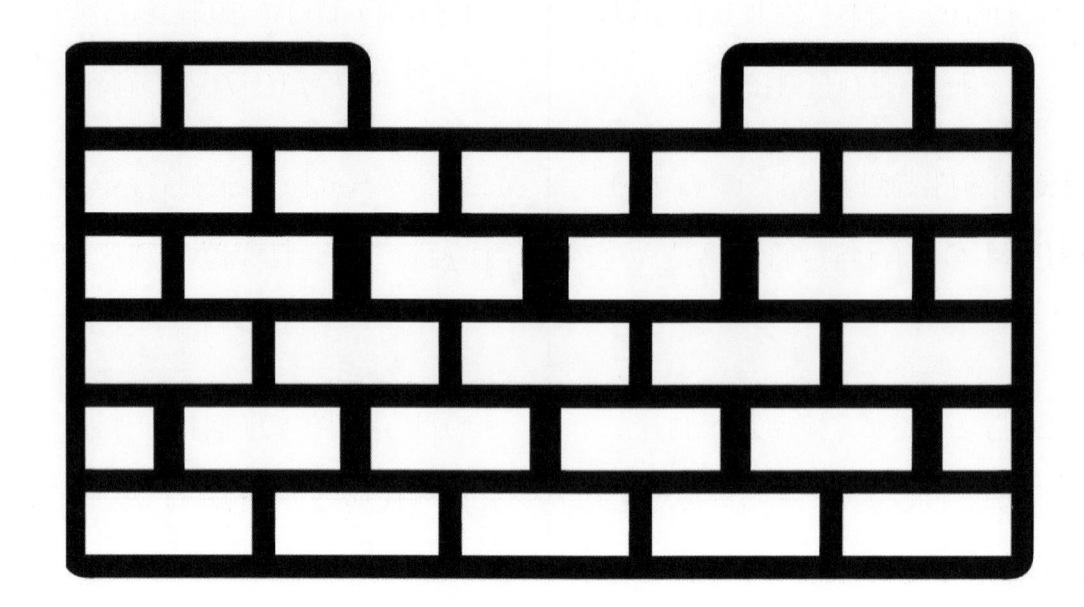

But Jesus can SMASH down the wall! Draw the smashed wall, and you and Jesus being best friends.

PHOTOCOPIABLE © www.joyvee.org

Born to be Super – Week 5   Worksheet 5.2

> *How can they call on one they have not believed in? And how can they believe in the one of whom they have not heard? And how can they hear without someone preaching to them?* Romans 10:14

To help:

We were made me remember for **Purpose**

We find it when we are **Close** to God

Selfish actions build a **Wall**

We can't **Smash** it, so Jesus came

He died as a **Punishment** to smash the wall

He came **Alive** again.

Dear Jesus, I'm sorry for all the bad things I did that stop me being close to You. I don't want those things between us anymore. Thank you for coming and smashing the wall. I want to be your friend. I want to live my life with you. Amen

Holy Spirit helps us

Dear Jesus, Thank You for being my best friend. Please send the Holy Spirit into my life to help me live for You. Holy Spirit, please come into my life, Amen.

Friends I want to pray for:
*
*
*
*
*

PHOTOCOPIABLE © www.joyvee.org

Born to be Super – Week 1 Teacher's Sheet 1

For Game 2, print and cut out the following instructions:

Introduce yourself to someone you don't know very well	Ask your teacher three questions and wait for their answers
Ask 4 people how they are and wait for their answer	Tell one of the helpers a verse from the Bible
Don't talk to anyone – after 1 minute you can sit in the completed corner	Sing 'God Save the Queen' – if you don't know, you need to ask someone to help you
Run around the room 3 times	Sing the first 4 lines of your favourite song
Try to stop 3 people from sitting in the corner – without touching them	Stand still like a statue until 3 people have spoken to you – then you are free
Turn all the lights off in the room	Hop around the room

PHOTOCOPIABLE © www.joyvee.org

Born to be Super – Week 1 Teacher's Sheet 1

You can't walk - try to find someone to give you a piggy-back or carry you to the corner	You cannot talk, but you need to make 3 people laugh without touching them
Run around telling everyone to stop the game	

PHOTOCOPIABLE © www.joyvee.org

Extract from chapter 7 of *Kai – Born to be Super*

'How do you know I had a dream?' asked Kai.

'Jesus told me,' Zoe shrugged.

'What, a voice from the sky? "Kai had a dream."' Kai used his biggest booming voice. Zoe giggled. Mr Clark looked across at them and smiled.

'No. It's more like a very quiet thought. When I'm asking Jesus about someone, I'll suddenly get a new thought about them, or maybe I'll see a picture of them in my imagination.'

'What d'you mean?' Kai asked.

'Last Wednesday, I kept thinking about the lady in the corner shop, Mrs Khan. Do you know her?'

Kai nodded. Mrs Khan always took time to talk and listen, especially to the children. She wouldn't let the adults push in front of them.

'Every time I thought of her, I kept seeing a picture of cake. It was strange. And every time I thought of cake, I saw Mrs Khan in my mind. So, I went home and told Mum. We decided to make her a cake and take it to her. It took all evening because I wanted to decorate it and make it really nice. We took it round just as she was shutting the shop. I gave her the cake, and she started to cry. It was her birthday, and everyone was so busy, they'd all forgotten.'

'Do you honestly think that Jesus knows about Mrs Khan's birthday?' Kai asked.

Zoe looked surprised at Kai's question.

'Of course He does. He knows everything. He knows when your birthday is, too.'

'Prove it! Get Him to tell you right now,' Kai glared at Zoe. Would Jesus really tell her?

'It's not like that, Kai.' Zoe shook her head. 'It's not a magic trick where Jesus tells me anything I want. He tells me the things that are important to Him.'

Zoe took a deep breath and looked Kai straight in the eye.

'He told me you were born to be super.'

PHOTOCOPIABLE © www.joyvee.org

Extract from chapter 9 of *Kai – Born to be Super*

'Does Jesus like to laugh?' As soon as he said it, Kai wanted to grab the words and pull them back again.

'Yes, He does,' Alison said, leaning against a wall. 'The Bible tells us He was "full of joy". Someone who is full of joy – I think they'd laugh a lot.'

Kai nodded. That made sense.

'What kind of things did Jesus do?' Kai asked, hoping it wasn't a silly question.

'He went from town to town, teaching people about God.'

Kai pulled a face. 'That sounds boring.'

'Well, He used stories about everyday things – funny stories.'

'Like what?'

'OK, imagine you are looking after a cat,' Alison said. Kai smiled. That was easy.

'Now you have three cats to keep an eye on.' Trickier, OK?

'Actually, it's ten cats. No, twenty cats.'

Kai could picture loads of cats around their feet, sitting in his backpack, climbing on Alison's head.

'Now it's 100 cats!' The story was becoming crazy.

Alison continued, 'Imagine one of them wandered off.'

'So what? How would I even notice?' said Kai. 'Do you think I'm going to go and find one cat when I still have all the others? That's silly! Who would do that?'

'God would! That's one of the stories Jesus told, but He used sheep, not cats.'

'So did God go and find the lost one, or did He stay with the rest?'

'He went after the lost one because it was precious to Him,' explained Alison. 'In the story, Jesus used sheep to mean people. God has lots of people He is looking after, but each one is precious, and He doesn't want anyone to be lost.'

'But what about the rest? Didn't He care about them?'

Alison looked thoughtful for a minute. 'Maybe they just stayed together. I think sheep are easier to look after than cats.'

'So, is that all Jesus did? Just tell stories?' Kai wasn't too sure about the cat or sheep story.

'Oh no. He did miracles.'

'Like what? Oh, I remember a story in the Bible about someone parting the sea so everyone could walk through. Was that Jesus?'

Alison frowned slightly. 'That was Moses. He lived before Jesus. But Jesus walked on water one time, and told a storm to stop, and it did. He also healed lots of people.'

PHOTOCOPIABLE © www.joyvee.org

Born to be Super – Week 6　　　　　　　　　　　　　　　Teacher's Sheet 6

GAME 1

Team A – Show the runner from Team A this photo
(Make sure no one else can see)

Team B – Give each runner from Team B a slip of paper

It is a building	There are six little windows
The bottom of it is red	It is tall
There are 2 red stripes	There are 2 white stripes
It has a big window at the top	It is on some grass

PHOTOCOPIABLE © www.joyvee.org

Born to be Super – Week 1   Parents' Letter 1

Dear Parents,

This week we have started to look at how we find our purpose in life by being friends with God.

Our Bible verse was:

> **For we are God's masterpiece. He has created us anew in Christ Jesus, so we can do the good things he planned for us long ago.** Ephesians 2:10 (NLT)

We discussed how ↓

Our Skills + God's Purpose = Superpower Impact!

If you want to help your child more at home, you can:
- ♦ **Pray** with them for God to reveal His purpose to them.
- ♦ **Share** with your child how God uses *your* skills to achieve His purposes.
- ♦ **Encourage** them to memorise the Bible verse.

This topic is based on the book 'Kai – Born to be Super' by Joy Vee. It is available anywhere books are sold, or you could request it at your local library. It is also available as a free e-book on all e-book platforms. It is not necessary for your child to read this book to participate in the class, but it is an additional resource if you wish to get it. This week's lesson covered Chapters 1-3

PHOTOCOPIABLE © www.joyvee.org

Born to be Super – Week 2   Parents' Letter 2

Dear Parents,

This week we looked at how God is close to us in difficult situations. Our Bible verse was:

> But now, O Jacob, listen to the Lord who created you.
> O Israel, the one who formed you says,
> "Do not be afraid, for I have ransomed you.
> I have called you by name; you are mine.
> ² When you go through deep waters,
> I will be with you.
> When you go through rivers of difficulty,
> you will not drown.
> When you walk through the fire of oppression,
> you will not be burned up;
> the flames will not consume you." Isaiah 43: 1-2

We have looked at these promises of God, and examples in the past. Sometimes, it doesn't feel like God is with us in difficult times. It is not always easy to hold on to the promises of God, but we need to remember that His word is stronger than our feelings.

If you want to help your child more at home, you can:
- **Pray** with them for God to reveal His purpose to them.
- **Share** with your child how God uses your skills to achieve His purposes.
- **Encourage** them to memorise the Bible verse.

This topic is based on the book 'Kai – Born to be Super' by Joy Vee. It is available anywhere books are sold, or you could request it at your local library. It is also available as a free e-book on all e-book platforms. It is not necessary for your child to read this book to participate in the class, but it is an additional resource if you wish to get it. This week's lesson covered Chapters 4-5.

PHOTOCOPIABLE © www.joyvee.org

Born to be Super – Week 3 *Parents' Letter 3*

Dear Parents,

This week we looked at how God speaks to us today.
Our Bible verse was:

> **When the Spirit of truth comes, he will guide you into all truth. He will not speak on his own but will tell you what he has heard. He will tell you about the future. ¹⁴ He will bring me glory by telling you whatever he receives from me.** John 16:13-14

We have looked at how God speaks to us through our thoughts and perceptions. We used a three-tool check – Is it **Kind**? Is it **Peaceful**? Does it **Point to Jesus**?

If you want to help your child more at home, you can:
- **Pray** with them for God to reveal His purpose to them.
- **Share** with your child how God uses your skills to achieve His purposes.
- **Encourage** them to memorise the Bible verse.

For more teaching on listening to God, you may want to get 'The Treasure Man' by Joy Vee and read it together as a family.

This topic is based on the book 'Kai – Born to be Super' by Joy Vee. It is available anywhere books are sold, or you could request it at your local library. It is also available as a free e-book on all e-book platforms. It is not necessary for your child to read this book to participate in the class, but it is an additional resource if you wish to get it. This week's lesson covered Chapters 6-8.

PHOTOCOPIABLE © www.joyvee.org

Dear Parents,

This week we looked at how we can talk about Jesus with our friends. Our Bible verse was:

> **Always be prepared to give an answer to everyone who asks you to give a reason for the hope that you have. And do this with gentleness and respect.** 1 Peter 3:15

We looked at different ways Paul talked to people about Jesus, depending on their background. We also looked at a story of Jesus, to see if we could retell it using modern examples, so our friends could understand it better.

If you want to help your child more at home, you can:
- **Pray** with them for God to reveal His purpose to them.
- **Share** with your child how God uses your skills to achieve His purposes.
- **Encourage** them to memorise the Bible verse.

This topic is based on the book 'Kai – Born to be Super' by Joy Vee. It is available anywhere books are sold, or you could request it at your local library. It is also available as a free e-book on all e-book platforms. It is not necessary for your child to read this book to participate in the class, but it is an additional resource if you wish to get it. This week's lesson covered Chapters 9-11

Born to be Super – Week 5 Parents' Letter 5

Dear Parents,

This week we looked at the gospel message.
Our Bible verse was:

> **How can they call on the one they have not believed in? And how can they believe in the one of whom they have not heard? And how can they hear without someone preaching to them?** Romans 10:14

We have looked at how we can break down the gospel message to simply share with our friends. If you want to discuss or help your children learn the points – this is how it was explained to them:

- God **created** everyone for a special purpose.
- We can only find our true purpose when we are **close** to Him.
- Our **selfish** things and wrong things – 'sins'- build a wall between us and God.
- God knew people are not strong enough to break down the wall, so He sent His Son, **Jesus**.
- Jesus came and lived a perfect life, but then He died as a **punishment** for our sins.
- But He didn't stay dead. He came **alive** again, **smashing** the wall, so we can be close friends with Him.
- You can say a prayer to get close to Jesus again – like this one:

Dear Jesus, I want to say I'm sorry for all the bad things I did, the bricks that made a wall between us and stopped me being close to You. I don't want those things between us anymore. Thank you for coming and smashing the wall. I want to be your friend. I want to live my life with you. Amen

- Now, you can live your life close to Jesus!
- But it's **not easy** remembering Jesus every day, and we need extra help. So, Jesus sends us the **Holy Spirit** who lives in us and helps us remember Jesus and teaches us how to be His friend.
- You can pray a prayer like this:

Dear Jesus, Thank You for being my best friend. Please send the Holy Spirit into my life to help me live for You. Holy Spirit, please come into my life, Amen.

- Now you can live the life you were born to live.

If you want to help your child more at home, you can:
- ♦ **Pray** with them for God to reveal His purpose to them.
- ♦ **Share** with your child how God uses your skills to achieve His purposes.
- ♦ **Encourage** them to memorise the Bible verse.

This topic is based on the book 'Kai – Born to be Super' by Joy Vee. It is available anywhere books are sold, or you could request it at your local library. It is also available as a free e-book on all e-book platforms. It is not necessary for your child to read this book to participate in the class, but it is an additional resource if you wish to get it. This week's lesson covered Chapters 12-15.

PHOTOCOPIABLE © www.joyvee.org

Dear Parents,

This week we talked about who the Holy Spirit is and had a round-up of our *Kai – Born to be Super* series.
Our Bible verse was:

> **The Holy Spirit, who the Father will send in my name, will teach you all things and will remind you of everything I have said to you. John 14:26**

Thank you for your support of your children through these weeks. Please continue to **Pray**, **Share** and **Encourage** your children on their walk with God.

Please check out Joy's other books, at www.joyvee.org, for more stories to help your children grow in God. You can also use the contact form to let Joy know what you and your children thought of Kai.

PHOTOCOPIABLE © www.joyvee.org